Search Engine Optimization and Marketing for Beginners

Renée Kennedy

Terry Kent

The Write Market

Search Engine Optimization and Marketing for Beginners

The Write Market

179 Vista Lane
Shenandoah Junction, WV25442

www.thewritemarket.com

Universal Publishers
Boca Raton, Florida • USA
2005

ISBN: 1-58112- 472-4

www.universal-publishers.com

Design by: Terry Kent

Notice of Rights

Notice of Liability

Acknowledgements

Thank you to Richard Klotch for editing this book.

Thank you to Mary Howard for your articles "How to Get Rid of a Beer Belly and Flabby Chest" and "Smoking While Pregnant" from *Ask Nurse Mary* published on the HealthCrazed.com web site.

Thank you to Shannon Edwards (CatoctinKettleKorn.com) and Nap Napowocki (HealthFitCounter.com) for having the courage to take the risks that allowed us to explore the frontier of Search Engine Optimization.

ii

Table of Contents

Introduction

Successful search engine optimization (SEO) techniques require strong organization. This book will provide you with a thoroughly tested, successful process to optimize your web site.

In order to implement the process yourself, you must have the ability to change the text of your web pages. You may also follow the process, develop your own content, and then have your webmaster implement the content for you.

This book will provide a *very brief* look at the following:

HTML – to recognize specific parts of a web page that influence SEO.

Basic web writing skills – important to selling your products or services once you get the traffic.

Navigational structure – like your visitors, search

engine spiders need an easy path to follow. (Search engine spiders are programs that crawl your web site to store them in a database for later retrieval by a search engine.)

PPC or Pay-Per-Click campaigns – these might be an important step after you have optimized your site for "organic listings."

While the topics listed above encompass different job skills and might even be done by several individuals, it is important to have a basic understanding of how they influence the optimization of your site. To that end, a list of resources is provided at the end of the book. These are valuable tools to help you understand these skills.

There is also a good glossary of terms at the end of the book. In fact, we might suggest that you quickly read through the glossary before you start to read the rest of the book. We're going to start using some of these terms straight off – so, for the next few hours, get ready to immerse yourself in the world of search engine optimization.

Good luck!

SEO Philosophy

The emphasis of this book is on "how to" optimize your site. However, it is important that we relate a little of our SEO philosophy or theory to let you know where we're coming from.

Have a little patience. We have been optimizing web sites for six years. We've seen sites rise and fall in the search engines; at times, we've seen fluctuations in ranks on a day-to-day basis. How do we handle this? The answer is "patience." You must be patient and allow the search engines to put your site into the database. Once in the database, you must be patient when the search engines change their algorithms and do funny things to your rankings. If you optimize using the techniques in this book, your site *will* weather the changes in search engine algorithms. Some search engines change their algorithms every other week! They do it in order to keep their data fresh and relevant. *This book does not* *reference or recommend chasing algorithms.*

Be persistent. By keeping accurate records and reviewing them on a weekly, or even monthly basis, you will enhance your chances of completing all necessary tasks. Persisting at these tasks will put you above your competition. First, you must be persistent with the focus of your site. Whatever you decide the theme or niche of your site will be, keep the focus and never let it slip from your grasp. Second, you must be persistent at getting your sites into search engine and directory databases. Third, you must persist at adding content to your site on a steady schedule. After you initially optimize your most relevant pages, content development will be a continuing task. We will cover this in detail in the last chapter.

Don't put all your eggs in one basket. We don't rely on any one specific search engine for traffic. Our optimization techniques will get your pages ranks in *all* search engines across the board. You may see some differences in individual ranks for specific keywords. However, you will also find that if you are fairly well-ranked in one engine, you will do fine in all the others, as well. *This book is not going to teach you about optimizing for specific search engines.*

In the same vein, we tell our clients that they cannot rely solely on search engines (whether pay-per-click or organic listings) to provide them a living. Search engines are merely one marketing method. *Our successful clients realize the necessity of implementing a marketing campaign that integrates offline methods of promotion with online methods of promotion.*

It takes time. Optimizing your web pages and seeing some real results is going to take time. *After submission, you should start to see results in about 2 months of time, maybe less.* If you haven't seen results within two months, something is wrong! There is a troubleshooting section and a checklist at the back of the book to help you work through these issues.

The more property you own the richer you are. Think of the Internet as a wild frontier. The more land of that wild frontier that you can stake a claim to, the richer you will become. *The more pages of optimized content you have, the more traffic you will get.* It only stands to reason that if you have more pages indexed by search engines, then you will have more chances to have those pages ranked. We've seen this assumption proved again and again so we're not shy about talking it up. Again, we will cover content development in the last chapter.

Before You Begin

Before you attempt the process of actually optimizing individual pages of your site, you will need to do several things to ensure that your site is ready for optimization.

Acquire your own domain name and hosting services. Search engines and especially directories are more likely to index pages in the root directory than pages in subdirectories of the server. Free web sites are placed in subdirectories (not in the root directory). Therefore, they have less of a chance of being found and indexed by search engines.

Hosting services can be obtained very inexpensively. You can find services as low as $3.95 per month. Do a search for "hosting" in your favorite search engine and you will find a multitude of choices.

Also, people visiting your site are more likely to trust

your offerings if they know you've invested in a real web site. *Having your own domain name and hosting service is imperative.*

Achieve a professional, attractive design. You should have a professionally designed template for your web site. This template may include a graphical navigation system and a familiar page layout. Professional designers are skilled at creating intuitive, user friendly, navigable sites. You need a site that people can learn to use quickly and easily.

This step is important for two main reasons:

> When you submit to directories, real people (humans, not machines) will visit your site and decide if it's worth including in the directory. *You cannot afford a shoddy design and lose the chance of getting into directories.* Directories are essential to search engine optimization. (More on directories later.)

> A quality, professional design entices people to buy your products. People trust a well-designed web site with professional graphics. People will not trust something made by your half uncle's brother's best friend who is dabbling in web design.

With that said, professional layout and graphics do not have to be expensive. There are plenty of sites that now offer free, professionally designed web site templates.

Do a search in your favorite engine for "free web site templates."

Ensure that your site has proper navigation. Proper navigation allows search engine spiders to follow your links and put your pages into their database. People need to find their way around your site, as well. Sometimes, organization is what distinguishes a high quality site from a loser. A well designed navigational system will have a positive impact on search engine optimization.

Write and develop your content. *Content is King.* All search engines, directories, or otherwise, will index your web site based on CONTENT. ALL of them. Content is the key to developing an Internet presence.

You will build a good reputation with high-quality content. If you have interesting content other webmasters will want to link to your site. (Obtaining links into your site is a priority for SEO. More on links later.)

Also, your content must be focused. Content that works around one theme will help you attract your target market. You will attract attention to your site if you can become a respected provider of information about your niche.

For instance, thewritemarket.com provides a wealth of information on web marketing. We try to stick to topics of design, marketing, and promotion – information that we feel would be useful to consumers looking for web design services. The content has drawn attention to our site and our services. The content helps us sell our services because people trust that we are experts in our field.

The purpose of this book is to help you write your content in ways that both people and search engines can understand.

Download or Bookmark the following tools. (We cannot guarantee the continued availability of these tools):
- Google Tool Bar with Page Rank: available at google.com
- Link Popularity Check: available at checkyourlinkpopularity.com
- Invest in a stats program. If you are a beginner, we highly recommend Advanced Logger: perlonline.com
- Bookmark keywordcount.com
- Bookmark overture.com
- Check out webposition.com – this is a tool that can help you determine what keywords you are getting listings for. The program is useful, but it must be used wisely and sparingly.

Subscribe to the following free newsletters. (We cannot guarantee the continued availability of these ezines):
- High Rankings Advisor: highrankings.com
- Search Engine Guide: searchengineguide.com
- Search Engine Watch: searchenginewatch.com

The above are the best ezines on search engine marketing that we have found. They will take approximately 1-2 hours per month to read. We highly recommend that you subscribe to them in order to stay abreast of what is going on in the field of SEO.

There are also many discussion boards that you may be interested in. You will find a few of these in the resources section. However, after you gain knowledge and achieve a level of confidence in your SEO techniques, you may find that the boards become repetitive. We highly recommend them if you are a beginner. You may find a point where you want to give them up, or you may find yourself becoming a permanent fixture in their communities.

Writing Strategies

In the last chapter, we recommended that you write your web pages and develop your content before you begin the process of optimization. You will find that most of the following strategies contain a familiar theme. They are all about readability. Surprisingly, they are also strategies that will help get your pages ranks in search engines. *If you follow these strategies, half the battle of optimizing will be won.* We have found that pages written in this manner do very well in obtaining organic listings.

Write in "chunks." Don't overwhelm visitors with too much information in one paragraph. Present information in neat, readable chunks. If you chunk, your paragraphs will be about two to three sentences each.

Use headlines. Headlines are another way to make your pages more readable. In the past, using keywords in headlines or heading tags in the HTML was a recommended technique for optimizing your page. We still think it's a worthwhile technique.

Use lists. Lists allow visitors to scan your pages quickly, as well.

Bold. Bolding is best used to highlight important information. Bolding keywords is another technique that may help your optimization efforts, as well.

Do *not* use underlines for web text. Underlines should be reserved only for hyperlinks. Underlining text may confuse your visitors. Does it annoy you when you try to click on underlined text that goes nowhere? Why would you want to annoy your visitors?

Write at an eighth grade reading level. You want to make a web page easy to read. That doesn't mean that it shouldn't be interesting. While you need to keep your visitors excited about your content, many people don't have time to read involved text. If you need to include detailed explanations of your product, save them for pages deeper in the linking structure. Even so, always explain things to people in as simple a way as possible. Your first priority is getting visitors interested. For an example of this type of writing, read a newspaper. Newspaper stories are generally written at an eighth grade reading level.

Use the Inverse Pyramid. Write your most important

information first. Again, the newspaper story is a good example of this format. This format allows people to read only the first few paragraphs of a story to get the main facts. On the Web, you want to do the same thing: present the juiciest information first. This way, people can quickly scan the first few sentences of the page to see if it contains the information they are looking for.

Using the Inverse Pyramid style of writing has an advantage in search engines, as well. Some search engines will not "read" the entire page. Although this is changing and many search engines are now programmed to read the whole page.

Write it the way you say it. Write conversationally. *Talk to yourself!* Having trouble getting something on paper? Dictate, using a tape recorder. Verbalize what you want to say on your web page into the tape recorder - then transfer that to the web page.

Also, write as if you are talking to one person, not to a group of people. Use the word "you." For example, "Do you have trouble finding the time to read a good book?" Avoid phrases like, "Many people never have time to sit down and read a book." Make it personal.

Focus on your customers. Once you have figured out who your customers are, focus your writing on them. Write just for them. For instance, if your customers are webmasters, your writing may include words that webmasters understand - words like "server," "host," and

"FTP." If, however, you are targeting people with no knowledge of the web, seriously think about your language. If you are writing to mechanics or gardeners or the hip-hop culture, use their lingo and discuss the benefits of your product in a way they would understand and relate to.

Other writing strategies to help your customers stay interested:
- Use punctuation (- . , ! " % $ & ~ : to name a few). The em dash (—) can be very powerful — leading people to the next bit of text. Get a little creative.
- Use colorful, positive language. Use words that evoke emotion or motivate people.
- Paint images with words. Use comparison and adjectives to create pictures in people's minds.

Tell stories. Telling stories can help people relate a concept to their real lives.

Is your page neat? After you finish writing a page, walk away from it for a few minutes. When you come back to the page, does it look neat and orderly or messy and unreadable? Do certain words or phrases stand out? Are those the concepts that you want to stand out? Scan the headlines. Do they make sense? If people just read the headlines will they get the gist of the page?

Proofread. If you're not sure if you can proofread, hire someone. It's the best thing you'll ever do for your site.

Nothing turns someone off faster than glaring spelling errors. If your copy is sloppy, people may think your company is sloppy. Also, if your readers are concentrating on your errors, they may miss your message completely.

Web copy is never finished. The advantage of the Web over "hard" media is that it's never written in stone. A click and a save and it's changed. Keep going over your web copy. There's always something you can improve.

Navigation Strategies

Developing a link structure that works for both visitors and search engines is a skill. If you're interested in learning more about navigation, we highly recommend Steve Krug's book, *Don't Make Me Think!*

Navigation is of utmost importance to the "crawlability" of your site. Search engine spiders need to be able to crawl your site as easily as your visitors find their way around. Sometimes, what will work for your visitors, will not work for search engine spiders. The best advice we can give in this area is to keep your link structure as simple as possible. Simplicity may involve giving up certain ideas that you might have for the design of your site.

Flash, frames, CGI, or any dynamic pages (pages that bring in content on the fly) are some types of programming that may hinder the crawlability of your site.

Although, workarounds can be made. If the usability of your site depends on advanced programming, you can see our troubleshooting section for more information.

However, if you're a beginner, we recommend sticking to simpler programming methods for the navigation of your site. Plain old HTML text and image links are the best method.

Also, keep as much code off your pages as you can. Use relative links to your Cascading Style Sheets (CSS) and put your JavaScript in a separate .js file. (It is not the intent of this book to teach you these techniques, but you can learn about them through most HTML books or web tutorials. See the resources section.) Linking each page out to your scripts and styles will speed up the loading of each page. It will also allow the spider to get to your real text faster.

If you do plan on keeping your navigation fairly simple, here are some strategies that can help:

Your web copy needs to *lead* your visitors to the sale. It needs to pull them down the page, forcing them to scroll, because they want to read what comes next. And at the bottom, it must make them want to click to the next page or order.

Before you begin to think about your link structure, determine the goal of your site. In other words, what are you trying to achieve with your site? What information will you need in order to achieve these goals?

Organize the information. The link structure will emerge as you write your web copy. Develop individual pages that provide clear information. Standard pages might include:

Home – a welcome page explaining what people can find at your site, might show some featured products.

Products and/or *Services* – these pages might be the entrance to your product catalog and may contain a categorized list of your offerings.

Guarantee – your policy for guaranteeing your customer's satisfaction.

Testimonials – good things other people are saying about your products or your company.

FAQs – if you have a lot of interactivity on your site, you might need some FAQ pages (Frequently Asked Questions.)

About Us – how your company was started, interesting facts about your company, possibly your mission statement, a little about different people in your company.

Contact Us – how people can get in touch with your company. Give them many options including email, phone, postal address, and fax.

Resources – links to other web sites and interesting articles that relate to your industry. This section is extremely important to building the content that will allow you to continue expanding your search engine promotion. We will discuss this in greater detail in the last chapter.

Order Now – ordering system. Give people as many options as possible for payment including credit cards, check, cash or money order. Give them options for processing the order including online credit card and check processing, phone and fax ordering.

Link structure must be carefully planned. First determine your *Main Navigational Links*. Using a template will help you ensure that you have your main navigational links on every page. These links will generally be graphical links made out of images, not text links. They should either go across the top of the page or down the left hand side. *We recommend a maximum of 10 main navigational links.* A few more won't hurt, but try to realize your visitors need to find what they need and find it quickly.

After your main links, you may need to break your site down into sub categories or *Sub Navigational Links*. Your site may be divided into several sections; each of these sections would be accessible by a main link. From the main link, the section would break down into its own set of navigational links. For instance, the "About Us" section may be composed of several sub pages including "Mission Statement," "President," "History," etc. This second-level list of pages is called sub navigation. *Generally, if your Main navigation goes across the top of the page, then your Sub navigation would go down the left of the page.* If your Main navigation goes down the left, then your Sub navigation would go across the top.

Your second-level directories may lead to third-level and even fourth-level directories, especially if you have a product catalog that you need to organize by categories. *The main point to remember is that if your visitors can easily find what they are looking for, chances are that search engine spiders can also find their way to all your pages.* When trying to achieve organic listings, you must try to get most of your pages spidered and put into the search engine database. This is why navigation is so very important.

How Search Engines Work

What is a search engine? Search engines are the primary tools of Internet users for finding products, services and information over the web. Search engines allow people to search the entire Web (or at least those pages of the Internet that are in the search engine's database.)

How does a search engine index web pages? There are four parts to an engine that you need to know about for optimization purposes:

- *The spider* is a program that goes out across the internet, looks for and gathers up web pages.
- *The database* is where the spider will store the pages that it finds.
- *The search engine website*, e.g. google.com, is where searchers go to pull up information from the

database.

- *The algorithms* are programs that determine which sites will come up when searchers type in a query at the search engine website.

There are two ways that your site can get into the database:

- The spider will automatically find your site from a link on someone else's site.
- You submit your URL so that the spider will come out and find it.

What happens when I submit my URL to a search engine? First, the search engine's spider visits your URL immediately and schedules your page for inclusion in the search engine's database.

Second, usually within a few weeks, the spider comes along and places your page(s) into its database. There is no telling how many pages deep the spider will crawl or how many pages it will place in the database. Usually, on the first time around, it will be only a few pages - possibly only the home page.

Third, the spider revisits your page(s) to grab any changes you've made. (The old term for this was "automatic update.") Once a page is in the database, the spider usually revisits every few weeks. The spider will also begin to crawl your site more deeply and place more and more of your pages into the database.

Fourth, when people use a search engine, they type key-words into a search box on the search engine's website. They are submitting a query. The search engine, depending on algorithms, will pull up all of the sites relevant to that query.

What if I don't want a page indexed by a search engine? If you want to prevent a search engine from indexing a page, use the following tag in between the HEAD tags: <META NAME="robots" CONTENT="noindex">.

Better yet, create a text file named "robots.txt" in Notepad. To exclude all spiders from your site put only the following into the file:

User-agent: *
Disallow: /

To exclude only certain spiders from your site (you will need to know the names of the spiders that are associated with each search engine if you want to do it this way, e.g. Inktomi's spider is called Slurp):

User-agent: spider-name
Disallow: /

To exclude engines from certain directories or pages:

User-agent: *
Disallow: /somedirectory/

or

User-agent: spider-name
Disallow: /somedirectory/somepage.html

Then upload the robot.txt file to your root directory
where your top level web pages reside.

**Why would I want to exclude my pages from a search
engine?** Search engines may (or may not) penalize
pages or web sites that contain exactly the same content.
For instance, we have a client that has five web sites.
Four of the web sites are replications of the first web
site. We use the mirror sites for tracking various ad
campaigns. However, we don't want the search engines
to pick up all of the sites, they are exactly the same. We
only need the search engines to find the main web site.
Therefore, we use the robot.txt file:

User-agent: *
Disallow: /

We put this file in the root directory of the four duplicate
web sites.

Frankly, we cannot tell you for sure that search engines
will penalize duplicate sites. We've heard arguments
both ways. However, if you have a page ranking in the
engines, you don't want to mess with it and try duplicat-
ing the content on another web site or another web page.
We have no proof that the duplicate page could be injuri-

ous to the original page, but search engines are continually finding ways to combat spam. In the search engine's eyes, a duplicate page may look like spam. Therefore, the best thing to do is to avoid looking like spam.

Here is another bit of philosophy. People call and say, "What is the quickest way into a search engine? I need to get some ranks NOW." Some are desperate to try anything, including spam. When we hear that desperation in their voice, we say several things to them up front:

- There is no quick way to get organic search engine listings.
- Organic search engine marketing takes time and persistence.
- We cannot guarantee ranks on any specific keyword (although we are good at getting keyword phrases into the top ten on most of the engines).
- We cannot guarantee when your site will start to rank for keywords (although generally it takes about 2 months).
- We can guarantee that we do not spam the engines. *Our methods will help your site stand the test of time.*
- Our search engine marketing practices are based on the concept that "Content is King." In other words, it's all about the words on the page.
- Search engines are only one method of marketing, you should be applying several marketing

campaigns both online and offline to get the best value from your site.

What is the difference between a search engine and a directory? A search engine is a machine - or a *robot*. A human may program algorithms for a search engine, but humans have nothing to do with your site when the spider is visiting your site or when the engine is ranking your pages. Google.com is an example of a search engine.

Humans compile directories. Dmoz.org (Open Directory Project) is an example of a directory. When you submit your site to Dmoz, a human will review your site for consideration in the Dmoz directory of web sites.

A search engine has a very large database because it will store several pages of every web site it indexes. A directory will only store a link to the home page of each site and a description.

Search engines will take the description either from some of the sentences on the web page or from the description meta tag. A directory will take the description from your submission information. (More on how to submit later.)

Each major *search engine* is usually associated with a *directory*. For instance, when you go to Google and you type in a search, you are getting results from all the web sites stored in Google's database. However, Google's algorithms are also programmed to place emphasis on sites that are also listed in the Dmoz directory. In fact, Dmoz feeds results to most of the popular search engines, with the exception of Yahoo.

It is imperative that you are listed in all the directories associated with all the major search engines. Currently, those directories are Dmoz and Yahoo.

All search engines are related. Each search engine will use results from other search engines or directories. (It is unwise for us to expound on the exact relationships between all of the search engines and directories, because we're sure it will change by the time this book goes to press!) Go to BruceClay.com and take a look at the *Search Engine Relationship Chart*[TM] for the most up-to-date relationships.

Is it important that you know all of the affiliations? Not really. Just as this book does not advocate chasing algorithms, we don't suggest chasing search engines, either. You will eventually be found in all search engines, regardless of relationships. In fact, it is to your benefit that the search engines are related, because if you can get your site ranking in one engine, you will eventually be found by the others, as well.

Why do they all interrelate? Every search site wants to have the freshest data on the Net. Some of them compete for the biggest index of sites on the Net. If they draw from different sources, it helps them maintain a fresh database and a large one. However, just because two engines both take information from the same database does not mean that they rank that information in the same way. Also, it is a safe assumption that web surfers will find a particular search engine and stick with it. They learn how to use it; they become familiar with it. The interrelations between search engines and directories do not matter to the average surfer. The average surfer wants fresh content.

It is also possible that a surfer would like to go to an engine and get different content every time. Several engines have been known to rotate algorithms. This means that today you may type in a keyword and bring up a specific set of web sites, then (perhaps the following day), you type in the same keyword and bring up a totally different set of results.

You cannot worry about what the search engines are doing with their algorithms. It is more to your advantage to create content-rich pages that each focus on one or two particular keywords. In other words, look at the things on your site that are in your control, do not worry about what you cannot control.

What is stemming? Some engines use stemming technology. This means that sometimes a search engine will not only search for the words people type in, but also for words that are similar. For instance, if you type in "educational wooden toys," the engine might also look for "educational wood toy." The engine may do this if it cannot find good results for the terms that were queried.

Variables That Affect Ranks

This is a list of all the variables currently and previously known to affect search engine ranks. You should understand that some of these variables are more important than others.

Variables that affect ranks in a positive way (these factors probably will not change over time, these are the most important variables):

- Keywords in the text of the page. The one variable that ALL search engine algorithms take into account are the visible words on a web page. Therefore, your writing is the most important part of how a search engine ranks your pages.
- Link popularity.
- Keywords in the title tag.
- Listings in directories.

Variables that affect ranks in a negative way (these factors probably will not change over time):

- Spamming by using the same word or phrase several times in your title, meta tags, or text.
- Spamming by putting words or phrases into your meta tags or title that have nothing to do with the actual content people see on your web page.
- Using text the same color as the background.
- Using tiny text (font size "-1" or smaller) as a way to cram keywords into a page.
- Linking out to sites that have nothing to do with the focus or niche of your site.
- Linking out to link farms or free-for-all (FFA) link pages. (Sites that contain pages just for the purpose of exchanging links with other sites without concern for content. Generally link farms or FFA link pages have thousands of links and the links are added by means of a program not a human.)
- Links coming in from link farms or FFA link pages.

Variables that have been known to affect ranks in the past (these factors may change over time depending on the way the algorithm is programmed):

- Keywords in the domain name separated by hyphens or underscores, e.g. wooden-boats.com
- Bolding keywords, e.g. wooden boats
- Using keywords in heading tags, e.g. <H4>Wooden Boats</H4>
- Keywords closest to the top of the page.
- Keywords in the description tag.

34

- Keywords in the keywords tag.
- Keywords in the names of linked pages and in the linked words, e.g. <a href="wooden-boats">wooden boats</a>.
- Keywords in alt tags.
- Keywords as names of images, e.g. <img src="wooden-boats.gif" alt="wooden boats">.
- Getting listings in Pay-Per-Click search engines like Google Adwords or Overture.

A Sample of HTML

The following page contains a sample of a very simple HTML page. When optimizing, it is important to focus on the text that we've bolded. However, all of the text throughout the page will also help you achieve optimization.

EXAMPLE:

```
<HTML>
<HEAD>
<TITLE>Toy wooden boats, hand crafted and educational for your
child.</TITLE>
<META name="Description" content="Toy wooden boats are an educa-
tional gift.  Surprise your child with a handcrafted wooden boat.">
<META name="Keywords" content="toy wooden boats handcrafted
educational child children boat">
</HEAD>

<BODY BGCOLOR=#FFFFFF text="#000000" link="#663333"
vlink="#CC6600">
<blockquote>
<font face="Arial, Helvetica" size="3">
<center>
<h2>Toy Wooden Boats</h2>
</center>
<img src="toy-wooden-boat.gif" width="150" height="200" hspace="10"
border="0" alt="toy wooden boat" align="left">

<b>Toy wooden boats</b> have been proven through the years to
encourage educational activities.  These educational toys help teach
young children motor skills and imaginative games.
<p>

Our toy wooden boats are handcrafted out of pine.  They are hand
painted with acrylic, non-toxic paints and are sturdy enough to with-
stand play in water.
<p>

The boats are 12" in length and come with five wooden blocks that can
be used as cargo.  Playing with these blocks will help your child devel-
op motor skills.
<p>

Your child will have hours of fun with our handcrafted toy wooden
boats.  They make an educational gift that your child will enjoy.
<p>

<center>
<a href="wooden-boats.htm">Order Online</a>
</center>

</font>
</blockquote>
</BODY>
</HTML>
```

Link Popularity

What is link popularity? Remember back in school when some kids were more popular than others? Some kids seemed to have all the luck! On the Internet, you are in for the toughest popularity contest of your life, the success of your website in search engines will depend upon it.

The popularity of your site is determined by the following variables:
- The number of web sites linking to your site.
- The popularity of those sites linking to your site.
- The similarity of the content on sites that link to your site.

Why is link popularity important to search engine optimization? Currently, some aspect of link popularity is being used in all search engine algorithms. Hypothetically, if you have two sites that have equal content, then the site with more popularity will rank higher.

Link popularity is determined separately by each search engine. Yahoo may calculate a high popularity for your site, whereas Google may calculate a low popularity for your site. Each search engine may also use the popularity information in different ways. It depends on their specific algorithms.

Directories can help your link popularity. The more popular a site is that links to you, the higher in popularity your site will be rated. The most widely used directories, Yahoo and Dmoz, are very popular. A listing in one of these directories will have a positive impact on your popularity.

What is click popularity? You may hear the term "click popularity." We haven't seen the click popularity variable used recently to determine ranks (except perhaps Google Adwords) but here is a brief explanation.

Click popularity is the number of clicks your site gets when it comes up in a search. So if your site is Number 3 for a search, and it is being clicked on more often than Number 2, you can potentially move ahead of Number 2. In order to increase click popularity, your title and description are of utmost importance.

Who is linking to you? There are several free tools available to check your link popularity. We like *Link*

Popularity Check available at checkyourlinkpopularity.com. It will compare your link popularity to your competitor's link popularity. It isn't necessary that you keep an eye on your competitor's link popularity. In fact, it can get downright maddening at times. However, you may find it useful to see how your site is progressing.

There are other tools available to check your popularity in specific search engines, check out the resource section for more of these tools.

Also, you can usually type your domain directly in the search engine to figure out how many inbound links your site has (yourdomain.com or www.yourdomain.com or link:yourdomain.com)

There are two ways to increase popularity. Here's the section you've been waiting for! How do you get all those cool, popular sites to link to your site? The number one answer is content.

Good sites provide good resources. A good resource may be a link to another website. Good sites have good webmasters that know the benefit of linking. The Internet is a Net or a Web of interrelated sites. Originally the internet was developed by the government, colleges and universities to share vast amounts of information. It quickly expanded to include other entities such as businesses, charities and individuals. This global sharing of information occurs through linking.

Here are some strategies for building content that other webmasters will be eager to link to:

- *Focus:* On your site, provide web pages of content specific to a niche of information. For instance, if you are in the business of selling toys, you will need to provide information on and about children's toys. If you start providing off-topic content, you will only serve to confuse visitors and search engines. When your site starts to grow with a range of content on a specific topic, other webmasters will start to find you in the search engines and they will start to link to you.
- *Unique:* Providing unique information about your niche will give you a big advantage. Providing unique products or services in your niche will give you a marketing advantage.
- *Mass Quantities:* Providing a gross amount of information about your niche in an organized format will also give you an edge over the competition.

You might also consider harvesting links. This is usually called a "reciprocal links campaign." Basically, you will need to solicit other webmasters and *ask* for a link. Here's the process:

- Do a search for sites that relate to yours.
- When you find a site with similar or complimentary content, look for a links page. If they don't offer a links page directly off their home page, move on.

- If they have a links page directly off the home page, then the next step is placing a link to their site on your site.

- Then contact them via email, tell them you've placed a link to their site, give them the exact page URL where their link is located. Give them a title, URL and description for your site.

- If you don't hear back from them, it is not necessary to remove their link from your site. You should be building a links page with links to some good resources, anyway.

You have to be careful with a reciprocal links campaign. You don't want your links section to turn into a "link farm." The pure way to get people to link to you was mentioned above – content. You can't begin a reciprocal links campaign with the mentality that you are only trying to get links in. *Go into it with the mentality that you are trying to provide resources for your visitors.* Don't worry too much about what the other webmasters are doing. Do worry about what you are doing and who you are linking to.

Considerations when linking to other sites:
- Be conservative. If a site looks shady or ill-designed then don't link to it. If it even resembles a link farm or an FFA page, don't link to it.

- Don't link off your site from your home page. Design a links page or resources page for the sole purpose of linking off your site. Or if you are providing articles or other types of information you may want to link off on the article page to provide further resources for your visitors.

- Don't link off your site on your product or services pages. You should be using your product catalog to sell your stuff. Linking off to other sites could distract your visitors from the main purpose of your site – to make sales.

Thewritemarket.com is a real-life example of how to achieve link popularity. In 1998, we set up thewritemarket.com. One page of the site was dedicated to linking out to other sites - a simple links page. We wanted these links in one place for quick access for our own use. All of the links that we put on this page related to our industry. As we continued to add links, we started to think about what would also be useful to our visitors. Eventually, we had to expand and categorize these links. The resource directory now contains about 10 pages of links.

In 1999, we started to write articles about our industry. These articles developed into tutorials. Many other people found these articles, tutorials, and links useful. Other webmasters started to link to our site because of the free content we were providing. We did not need to solicit links, they happened as a natural reaction to the content. This is the way it is supposed to be. Search engine algorithms are programmed to rank popular sites higher because popular sites should be valuable.

Currently, we field about ten requests per week from

other webmasters asking for reciprocal links. At this point, we no longer link out to other sites unless it is an exceptional resource.

At some point, your site will reach a point of saturation. At this point, the only way you will be able to increase your link popularity is by obtaining a link into your site from an extremely popular site.

For instance, we were promoting a client's site with a Google "page rank" of 5/10. (Google page rank is an indication of a site's popularity and how that site will rank in Google listings. You can see your Google page rank if you download the Google Toolbar. Ten is a great page rank. Zero is the worst page rank.)

We were able to increase the client's site to a page rank of 7/10 by purchasing a link from the CNN web site to the client's site. The CNN site had a page rank of 10/10. This link increased the overall popularity of the client's site to gain an increase in traffic of about 500 unique visitors per day (not solely from the CNN link, but traffic from all search engines). However, we believe that this significant increase in traffic was also dependent on the fact that the site was in the weight management niche. (65% of the US population is overweight, making weight management a red hot niche.)

If you are trying to market to a niche that is lukewarm, you will never see this incredible leap in traffic because there just aren't that many people interested. (For instance, maybe your product is a tool for electricians.)

The lesson is that no matter what your product/services are, you've got to increase your link popularity in a cost effective manner. You must take into consideration the time, money and niche market involved. What may work splendidly for one market will be a total failure for another. Sometimes, you need to be willing to take calculated risks to discover what internet marketing techniques will work best for *your* business.

The next section will describe an optimization process that will benefit *all* websites, regardless of niche.

Writing for Search Engine Promotion

At this point, you should realize that search engine optimization is all about the words on your web page. The following sections will give you a step-by-step process to improve your writing for the benefit of both your visitors and search engines.

Step 1: Write Content. We've already stated that your content is the most important part of search engine promotion. Before you begin to optimize your page, you need to have some text on the web page. Your content and navigation are related, so some of the content will be created while you're developing link structure.
However, some content will need to be developed after your navigation is in place. If this is the case, here are some ideas for writing a web page:

- Get your main ideas down. Ask yourself some questions:
  - ❯ What is the goal of this page? In other words, what do I want to get out of this page?
  - ❯ Who do I want to come to this page?
  - ❯ What would those people want to read?
- Organize the page by using headers, lists and other tactics in the section "Writing Strategies."
- Write about 100-300 words on the page.
- Try an outline, then begin to fill it in with natural, conversational writing. If you're having trouble getting something on the page, try writing it as if you were explaining it to someone. Pretend you're talking to someone and put those words on your page. Brainstorm, just let your ideas flow, you can fix the details later.
- This is a rough draft. Don't expend a lot of energy making it sound wonderful. You are going to have to rewrite it several times, anyway.

Step 2: Find keywords. Before you begin to rewrite the content of your web page to increase or decrease keyword frequency, you must find the *right* keywords. If you are only optimizing one site, we recommend keeping a list of keywords and keyword phrases right in this book. There are a few pages at the very end of the book where you can start a list of keywords. Keep adding to your list when you find new words. This list will become a useful resource for optimizing your web site.

There are several ways to find keywords and you should strive to try all of these strategies:

- *Brainstorm.* Come up with at least 20 keywords or keyword phrases that you think people might type into a search engine in order to find your web pages. Use your knowledge about your industry, but try to remember to think like people that are looking for the types of products and services that you are offering.

- *Ask other people.* Ask business people and friends what they would type into a search if they were looking for your page or site. It is especially helpful to get the opinions of people outside of your industry, people that know little about your products and services.

- *Use the search engines.* Go to search engines and look for pages with content similar to your own. When you get to your competitor's sites, look at their source code. (Place your cursor on the page, click your right mouse button and choose "view source.") Check out the phrases they are using in the keyword meta tags (if they have them). If you find some new keywords, be sure to write them down.

- However, do not copy someone else's meta tags or text word-for-word. Plagiarism will be easily discovered. Also, copying someone else's text is not going to help you in the search engines. You will have more success providing original content.

• *Use a "keyword suggestion tool."* There are several keyword suggestion tools. Overture and Google Adwords have free ones. In order to find these tools, go into your favorite search engine and type in the query "keyword suggestion tool." They are extremely helpful to finding phrases that you probably never thought of.

Step 3: Target keywords. Once you have found several keywords and phrases, you will need to make sure they are targeted. If you pick a general (common) word that is highly searched, you are less likely to get a good ranking than if you pick a phrase that is less highly searched but more specific. For example, the keyword "toy" is too general. What kind of toys are you trying to promote? If you narrow it down to "educational toy" or "wooden toy," you have a better chance of getting a good rank (*good rank* means a listing in the top ten).

Getting very specific is important, not only for rankings, but also because you want people to find what you are offering. You don't want people to be annoyed when they get to your page because they were looking for something else. Many people are search savvy, they know how to get the most out of search engines. If they type in a general search on one word, chances are good that they won't find what they're looking for. People learn quickly that they need to type in several words to find exactly what they're looking for. *Therefore, you need to narrow in on very focused keyword phrases.*

For example, if you're selling wooden boats, you might choose the following keyword phrases:

- educational wooden toys
- educational wooden boats
- toy wooden boats

Google and most other engines are now using *stemming technology*. This means that if people type in a word like "education," Google may bring up similar words like "educational." What does this mean to your keyword choice? You should still go for keyword phrases that people will most likely type in. Stemming is more of a help to the searchers than to optimizers. You still need to focus on keyword phrases that are very specific. If "educational wooden toys" is what most people are typing in, then don't use "education wood toy." Use the exact words that most people are querying.

With the exception of plurals, exact wording may be found with the Overture suggestion tool. This tool will give you exact queries from Overture for the previous month. You need to play with it for a few minutes to see exactly what we're referring to. Also it will help to clarify much of what we've been preaching about content and focus!

Step 4: Write the title. Titles become the links that you see in the search engine when you perform searches. Search engines generally bring up about 10 - 25 titles per search. Under each title, you will see a description of the site.

Those titles that you see are generated directly from the <TITLE> tag in a web page. *It is extremely important to have a title on every page you want to promote in search engines.*

Write the title carefully. Not only must you use keywords, you must also make it interesting. Here are some guidelines:

- Look at your keyword phrases that you've decided on for a particular web page.
- In your title, include as many of the words from your keywords and keyword phrases as possible up to 10 individual words.
- Try to use each word only once.
- Think about stemming and similar words.
- Making the title catchy might be difficult, but try it anyway. The title is the first thing people see about your site. You want people to look further (the description is next) so the title has to grab them. Here are some tips:
  - ▶ Ask a question
  - ▶ Solve a problem
  - ▶ Solve a problem quickly: time
  - ▶ Solve a problem for a cheap price: money
- The first words you use in the title are the most important words to the search engine, so use your most important keyword phrases as near the beginning of the title as possible, especially if you have a long title.
- Most people use lower case letters to search, and some engines are case specific. Don't use all caps:

they are difficult to read. Make your title a sentence if you can, capitalizing only the first word.

- Try to keep the title to within 100 characters. Characters include spaces, punctuation and letters.

EXAMPLES:

<TITLE>Educational toys including wooden boats!</TITLE>

<TITLE>Wooden boats make educational toys.<TITLE>

<TITLE>Educational toys, discounts on wooden boats.</TITLE>

<TITLE>Antique silver earrings with genuine ruby gemstones.</TITLE>

<TITLE>How do I get rid of my beer belly?</TITLE>

---

or even more simply:

<TITLE>educational wooden boats</TITLE>

<TITLE>smoking while pregnant</TITLE>

<TITLE>ruby earrings antique silver</TITLE>

<TITLE>low fat party appetizers</TITLE>

Step 5: Write the description meta tag. Not every search engine will use the description tag all the time. However, sometimes they do. One explanation for this is if the engine cannot find the keywords on the actual page, then it may take the description. Generally, search engines seem to be taking words between the body tags to create the description of the page. This renders the description tag meaningless. However, the best thing you can do for your page is to include the description tag. If for nothing else, when you go back to the page at a later date, you can immediately read the description to figure out what the focus of the page is.

Here are some guidelines for writing the description:
- Think about these two questions:
  - ▶ What is this page about?
  - ▶ Who do you want to come to your page?
- Make your description simple and to the point. Use keywords if you can, but make it sound exciting! Explain what makes your site unique. If you can throw in a word like "free," "discounts," or "resources," do it here. Also, if you can solve their problems quickly, say so. People are always looking for bargains and quick solutions.
- Try to limit character count to 150.
- Put your most important info first, because some engines will cut off the description after the first 150 characters.

EXAMPLE:

```
<META NAME="DESCRIPTION" CONTENT="Offering educational toys,
wooden boats and puzzles. Free letter from Santa with purchase of
two or more toys! Online ordering and overnight delivery.">


<META NAME="DESCRIPTION" CONTENT="Wooden boats make edu-
cational toys for children of all ages. Online ordering and overnight
delivery.">


<META NAME="DESCRIPTION" CONTENT="Antique silver earrings in
many styles and inlays including ruby, emerald, opal and diamond.
Free delivery.">


<META NAME="DESCRIPTION" CONTENT="How to get rid of your
beer belly and flabby chest - Ask Nurse Mary.">


<META NAME="DESCRIPTION" CONTENT="What is the impact of
smoking while pregnant - Ask Nurse Mary.">
```

Also, simply repeating the title in a slightly different way works:

```
<TITLE>Low fat party appetizers</TITLE>
<META NAME="DESCRIPTION" CONTENT="New recipes for low fat
party appetizers.">
```

or

```
<META NAME="DESCRIPTION" CONTENT="Recipes for dieters includ-
ing low fat party appetizers.">
```

Step 6: Write the keywords meta tag. The keywords meta tag is another tag that may or may not influence your ranks. However, we always include this tag because when we go back to the page, it helps us remember exactly what we optimized for. When you're dealing with 20 or more pages per web site, you can easily forget what words you tried to optimize each page for. Keeping a record of the words in the keywords tag really makes sense from an organizational standpoint.

Suggestions for writing your keywords tag:
- Try not to use an individual word more than three times. This includes all forms (derivatives) of it. For example, "toy" and "toys" might be considered the same word by some engines because of stemming. It would be prudent to pick one of these words and stick with it on a particular page, then if you must account for the other word, use it on another page.
- Use keyword phrases, not just individual words.
- Try to limit your character count to 1,000.
- Use the most important keywords or keyword phrases first.
- Should you separate your keywords with commas? It's definitely not something you should get hung up on. If it helps you decipher your phrases, by all means, use commas.

Examples – any of the following would work, from intense to very simple:

EXAMPLES:

<META NAME="KEYWORDS" CONTENT="wooden boats, educational toys, educational wooden toys, wooden toys, boats, educational">

<META NAME="KEYWORDS" CONTENT="ruby earrings, antique earrings, antique silver earrings genuine ruby gemstones">

<META NAME="KEYWORDS" CONTENT="low fat party appetizers">

---

or repeat the title:

<META NAME="KEYWORDS" CONTENT="how do I get rid of my beer belly and flabby chest">

<META NAME="KEYWORDS" CONTENT="smoking while pregnant">

Step 7: Rewrite the content for keyword density.
Rewriting is perhaps the hardest part. While some search engines use meta tags, all search engines use words between the body tags to rank pages. The words in the body are under your control and can be manipulated in the same manner as the title. The title and the body text are the only two variables that directly influence SEO and are under your control.

Suggestions for rewriting your text:
- Reread the page, you should have approximately 100-300 words on the page. If you don't, go back

and add more text. If you have more than 300 words, that's just fine. Consider staying under 1,000 words, though, just for the sake of readability.

• Your writing should be natural, almost conversational. Remember, the number one thing you are trying to do is to speak to your audience.

• Once you are satisfied with the page and how the words sound, you can increase keyword density. Look for synonyms for your keywords within the text. Replace some of the synonyms with the actual keywords if you need to. Also try to keep some of the synonyms if you have enough text to work with. If you don't, then just use your keywords.

• Use keywordcounter.com to examine your keyword density. Anywhere from 3% to 10% will work for your individual keywords (individual keywords make up keyword phrases). If you see that your individual keywords are each showing up around 1% to 2%, consider adding more of your individual keywords to increase their frequency.

• Don't mass all your keywords together. You want your keywords spread throughout the text. "Toy boats, toy boats, toy boats," is not natural even though it is fun to have someone try to say it fast.

• In a heading tag, use the same keywords that you used in the title tag. Bold or strong some of your keywords in the body text. Heading tags and bold tags will help the search engines key in on the words that you use them on.

- Think about the proximity of your individual key-words. Strive to keep important phrases together. For example, we might use "educational wooden boats" rather than "educational boats."
- If you can't increase your keyword density within the actual text put the extra ones into your alt tags. Some search engines "read" alt tags. Consider placing keywords in linked text, as well.

The following examples show how title, meta tags, and body text work together to create a page that will rank well in all search engines. They include only the HTML tags that we feel will help your page.

These pages are actual pages from our web sites. If you check out your favorite search engine for the following queries, you may find the actual web pages that we're using as examples:
- low fat party appetizers
- how do I get rid of my beer belly
- smoking while pregnant
- marketing goals
- how to write a survey

<TITLE>Five Low Fat Holiday Party Appetizers</TITLE>
<meta name="description" content="Recipes for quick and low fat party foods.">
<meta name="keywords" content="low fat appetizers">

<h3>Five Low Fat Holiday Party Appetizers</h3>
by Renee Kennedy

Holiday foods are about different kinds of flavors that satisfy your taste buds. Here are some food picks - healthy, low fat, all easy to make:

Marmalade, apple butter, or whole fruit preserves served on low fat crackers with slices of gourmet cheese. (Be sure to read the back of the packages of cheese and crackers, look for low-fat options.)

Pears and low fat cheddar cheese. The sweet, tang of the fruit with the sharp taste of the cheese is a mixture that will please any palette. When serving, allow guests to slice their own fruit — this will keep the fruit from turning brown.

Ham and turkey are both low fat meats if you choose lean varieties. Here are a few special ways to serve them depending on the level of sophistication of your guests:

For kids: serve the meat in bite-sized chunks, also offer grapes and chunks of low fat cheese... let your guests pick up these healthy nuggets with toothpicks.

EXAMPLE 1 CONT'D:

For the older crowd: Buy deli slices of ham, turkey, and cheese. Roll them up, serve with a choice of small dinner rolls (onion rolls, plain, egg, whole wheat...). Add a selection of fancy mustard or any unique fat-free condiments. (Have some fun experimenting with fat free mayonnaise and/or yogurt and spices like chili, dry mustard, onion and garlic.)

Shrimp is a fabulous appetizer that has 100 calories per three oz, very little fat, and tons of protein! A less expensive option is imitation crab or lobster (made out of whitefish and flavored to taste like crab or lobster.) Serve with cocktail sauce and it tastes nearly as good as shrimp. Again, toothpicks come in handy for this appetizer.

Bruschetta...
Slice a loaf of French baguette bread into1/2 inch slices, place on a cookie sheet.
Dice 2-3 large ripe tomatoes.
Chop 1/2 - 1 cup of fresh basil.
Mix tomato and basil together, add a little salt and pepper if you like.
Put tomato mixture on the sliced bread.
Sprinkle with shredded low-fat mozzarella.
Broil about five minutes until cheese is bubbly.

You may also want to read **<a href="healthy-appetizers.htm">**Five Healthy, Easy Party Appetizers**</a>**.

END EXAMPLE 1

EXAMPLE 2:

`<TITLE>`How do I get rid of my beer belly and flabby chest?`</TITLE>`

`<meta name="description" content="Ask the Nurse - How do I get rid of my beer belly and flabby chest?">`

`<meta name="keywords" content="how do I get rid of my beer belly">`

`<h3>`How do I get rid of my beer belly and flabby chest?`</h3>`

Q.

I am a 22 yr. old male, 5-9 160lbs. I have a beer belly and a flabby chest. I am looking to lose the fat AND build upper body muscle.

I work in a brickyard doing physical work and I am confused about what to eat? I also work as a produce clerk in a grocery store (also includes physical work such as lifting heavy sacks of potatoes and boxes of fruits). When I get home I do sit ups and push ups, and if I have the energy, I walk for a mile or so.

I have also changed my diet to a low fat one. I eat a healthy breakfast, a diet frozen entree for lunch and dinner, depending on if I am working or not, consists of either another diet frozen entree or grilled fish. I snack on low fat bars, protein bars, fruits and veggies, and only drink water and juice. Should I change my diet? Do I need to eat differently when I am working in the brickyard or the supermarket? Will my diet and work routine help me lose weight and build muscles?

EXAMPLE 2 CONT'D:

A.

I don't see with the physical work you have described how you would not turn fat to muscle. How long have you been doing this physical of labor?

I have a couple suggestions.

Make sure you are eating proteins and lots of them like meat. If you are eating quality proteins and are avoiding sugar you will probably not have to worry about eating low fat. Too often people try to cut out fat and miss out on quality proteins in the process. Protein is vital if you are trying to build muscle.

Be sure and use good body mechanics during your work. Keeping your back strait. Bend with your knees instead of your back those types of things. You will actually last longer at your work (especially once you have strengthened your muscles) and will build more muscle and have less chance of injury to ligaments and joints.

Mary Howard is a Registered Nurse, mother of two, and enjoys natural gardening. Come visit her <a href="http://homegrownmo.bravehost.com"><b>Homegrown web site</b></a>

END EXAMPLE 2

```
<TITLE>Smoking while Pregnant</TITLE>
<meta name="Description" content="Ask the Nurse.">
<meta name="keywords" content="smoking while pregnant">
<h3>Smoking while Pregnant</h3>
```

Q.

I am 17 weeks pregnant. I smoke 10 to 15 cigarettes a day. I want to quit. Is it too late to quit or has the damage already been done?

A.

It would be best to consult with your doctor. but from my experience it is not too late to quit. It is just a bit harder to quit while pregnant. Many doctors just advise to gradually decrease your smoking to a few cigarettes a day. You can quit if you can do it gradually enough not to stress your unborn baby. The less nicotine you take in the better it is for your baby so smoking just a few cigarettes a day is definitely better than 10 to 15 a day.

As far as affecting the birth-weight of your baby that remains to be seen. That depends largely on your nutritional status as a whole. From what research shows each time you smoke a cigarette it decreases the blood flow (and therefore oxygen) to your baby so the less frequently you cause this change in your body the better it is for your unborn baby. If you quit too quickly and you experience "physical" (not emotional, psychological) withdrawal symptoms it can stress to your baby.

Mary Howard is a Registered Nurse, mother of two,
and enjoys natural gardening. Come visit her `<a href="http://home-grownmo.bravehost.com"><b>Homegrown web site</b></a>`

END EXAMPLE 3

EXAMPLE 4:

```
<TITLE>What are Marketing Goals?</TITLE>
<meta name="description" content="Definition of marketing goals">
<meta name="keywords" content="what are marketing goals">
```

What are Marketing Goals?

#1. Marketing goals must fit into your overall business goals.

#2. Marketing goals should be quantifiable, meaning, you can measure them.

#3. We've talked quite a bit about strategy. Your marketing goals will be achieved by implementing your marketing strategies. Every time you embark on a marketing campaign, you will use one or more strategies to launch and maintain that campaign. However, in order to tell if your strategies are doing anything, you need goals, and you need to be able to "measure" whether or not you are achieving those goals.

Goals Checklist:

Are they realistic?
Are they specific?
Are they measurable?

END EXAMPLE 4

<TITLE>How to Design a Survey</TITLE>

<meta name="description" content="Tutorials at The Write Market.">

<meta name="keywords" content="how to design a survey write market">

<h3>How to Design a Survey</h3>

The survey can be a powerful tool to figure out what your market needs and how you can market to them. Just the process of developing a survey will help you learn more about your target market.

1. <b>What are you trying to find out?</b> Be very specific. Write them down.
EXAMPLE:
Here are a few of the goals for our survey:
How do people find our product web page?
Do these people own their own business?
Do they work for a small business or a large company?
What is the level of their Search Engine Optimization knowledge?
Where do these people hang out on the Internet?
Why don't they buy our product today?

2. <b>Who will you ask?</b> Who will be your sample?
EXAMPLE:
We are going to ask the following people to fill out our survey:
People that come to our home page
People that come to our product page
People that read our newsletter
We are also using ads in various e-zines to get the word out about our survey.

EXAMPLE 5 CONT'D:

3. <b>What method of surveying will you use?</b>

Here are some choices from most expensive to least expensive:

Personal Interview - face-to-face interviewing – sometimes conducted in a mall or on the street.

Telephone - probably one of the most popular methods.

Mail - inexpensive, also there is no interference by an interviewer, so there is less bias.

Web based - only use if your target population would be online.

EXAMPLE:

We are going to use a web based survey, because most of the selling of our book will occur online. Also, the only people that would be interested in our book would be people online.

4. <b>Plan your research carefully</b>

Once you know who you're surveying and the type of method you will use:

Develop a time line - how long it will take from designing the survey to analyzing the data.

Do a cost estimate. You might break down cost by each step involved.

EXAMPLE:

Our survey will costs us nothing but our own time.

Timeline:

Jan 1 - Jan 20: write survey

Jan 20 - Jan 30: run a pretest

Jan 31: rewrite what needs rewriting

Feb 1 to Feb 18: implement survey, send out ads in e-zines that will run ads for free, put on web site home page and product page.

Feb 18 - Feb 28: analyze data and incorporate into marketing plan

EXAMPLE 5 CONT'D:

5. `<b>`Design the survey.`</b>`

Write the survey based on the method that you have chosen (Number 3 above.)

6. `<b>`Pretest.`</b>`

Pretesting will help you determine if the survey is easy to understand, if people are able to fill it out, and other problems that may occur. Rewrite the survey if you need to.

EXAMPLE:

We pretested our survey to about 15 people - friends and family, that we were fairly sure would respond.

Side Note: we were going to skip the pretest because it's a little bit of a pain. DON'T SKIP IT. It actually told us several things that were wrong with our survey.

7. `<b>`Test.`</b>`

Do the actual survey. Collect the data and put it into an organized format.

EXAMPLE:

Here is our `<a href="../survey.htm"><b>`survey`</b></a>` - as long as you're going to check out our survey - please fill it out!

8. `<b>`Analyze.`</b>`

If you're using quantifiable information you can analyze with statistics. However, expect to spend some time learning how to do statistics. If you're statistically challenged, perhaps you want to develop a more qualitative survey. If so, you will analyze using inferences and basic reasoning rather than statistics.

Your goals will dictate your questions and the answers to those questions will help you determine what you will do with your marketing plan and the marketing strategies that you choose to employ.

END EXAMPLE 5

How to Submit

There are two ways to get the search engine spiders to find your site. The first way, the best way, is through a link from someone else's web site. However, this may be unrealistic for a brand new site. The second way is to hand submit your site to each major engine and directory. The rest of this chapter will cover hand submission of your site.

Submit to the engines. You may have heard of programs that will submit your site for you or you may have seen offers like, "Submission to 100 search engines for $29.95." Stay away from them. Submission to the important engines will only take you 5 minutes. The most effective method of submitting is to go to each search engine and submit your main URL directly to the engine. (Your main URL is http://www.yourdomain.com.)

You only need to submit to the major search engines.

Remember how all search engines are related? If you submit to the major search engines, all the minor ones will pick you up. Here are the majors, listed in order of importance:

- Google
- Yahoo
- MSN
- AOL
- AltaVista
- Netscape

Currently, you can submit to all of these through two add URL pages, the one at Google and the one at Yahoo. That's it, it's that simple. Two submissions and you're done! I will provide the current URL's, however, these might change by the time the book goes to press:

- google.com/addurl.html
- search.yahoo.com/info/submit.html

If you cannot find these pages, then go to every search engine listed above and look around for *add your site, suggest your site, submit your site* or a variation thereof.

Once your home page is in the search engine database, the spider will begin to crawl your other pages, therefore it is not necessary that you submit any other pages. Also, once your pages are in the database, there is no need to resubmit.

How do you know if your home page is in the database?

Go to the search engine and type in your domain name: www.yourdomain.com. If your site does not appear or it says there is no information for that URL, then you are not in the database. If even one page comes up, then you are in the database and there is no reason to resubmit.

See the troubleshooting section for more specific information if your site is not in the database.

Submit to the directories. While there are many online directories, there are two majors that will have an immediate impact on your search engine positioning campaigns. *It is imperative that you get into the major directories if you are trying to increase your ranks in search engines.* The two majors are dmoz.org (Open Directory Project) and yahoo.com.

Yahoo is currently $299 per year. Tips for Yahoo:
- search.yahoo.com/info/submit.html
- Look for Yahoo! Express.
- Read their guidelines. Follow their guidelines to the letter.
- Do not try to submit to Yahoo until your site is completely ready. This means no "under construction pages," no broken links, a professional design, etc. Realize that you may lose your $299 if your site is not ready.

Dmoz is free. However, sometimes it can be difficult to get a listing. Tips for Dmoz:

- Again, make sure your site is ready.
- Do not submit your site more than once. The editors know when you've submitted more than once and they will consider you a spammer if you continue to submit the same site over and over OR if you submit to several different categories.
- Drill down through the categories before choosing a category to submit to. Spend some time surfing the directory. This point cannot be stressed enough: *become familiar with the directory before you submit.*
- Write a brief one- or two-line summary of your web site. If they ask for about 30 words or less, give them 30 words or less. Do not try to cram all your keywords into the description. Do try to include a few of your main keywords.
- The home page is the easiest page to get accepted. Consider submitting sublevels of your site if they have a lot of content on a particular theme.
- Problems: unfortunately, these human-edited directories can be problematic. If you've followed their guidelines and the above tips, and you still aren't getting listed within two months, you should politely ask why you aren't getting a listing. First, email the editor of the category you are trying to get listed in. If there is no editor for that category, email the editor directly above your category. Tell the editor the site you are trying to get listed and the

category you are trying to get listed in. Ask if there is anything you can do to help the submission process.

- Wait two weeks. If you receive no response, go to the next highest editor and state that you have already written a letter to the editor of your category. Keep after them, do it politely, and you will get listed.

Other directories can also help your search engine popularity. Find other directories that are specifically related to your industry or general business directories. Every link will help, unless it is from a link farm or FFA page. If in doubt, do not pursue the link.

Keep track. It's important to keep track of all your submissions. If you can't remember when and where you submitted, it will be difficult to figure out why your site is not listed. At the end of the book, we've provided a form for you to write in the date you submitted, the engines and directories you submitted to, and the date you verified that your site was listed.

Analysis

Is your primary goal in a search engine promotion campaign to increase overall traffic or to increase sales? The determination of your success will depend on your goals.

You will need to have the following statistics or metrics available to analyze your success:
- How many unique visitors you get each week
- The specific search engines that are sending you traffic
- How many hits each search engine is sending you
- The keywords people use to find your site
- What your ranks are for certain keyword phrases
- Sales per week

In order to get the above information you will need a traffic analyzer that will report your site statistics. We recommend Advanced Logger available at

PerlOnline.com for your site statistics. Currently, they charge a one time fee ($29.95) for this statistical program. You must install it on your web pages and in your CGI bin or have your webmaster do it for you. Although Advanced Logger will not be as good as WebTrends, Urchin, ClickTracks, or HitBox, it will give you a lot of bang for your buck. It's a good tool for the beginning optimizer. You may decide to grow into a more expensive program when you become more experienced.

You will also need to be able to integrate your site statistics with your sales/week. You can use Microsoft Excel for this purpose. You can transfer some of the information from Advanced Logger into an Excel file that also contains your average sales/day over a week. This will give you some revealing statistics about the relationships between search engines, visitors, and sales.

Here is an example of such a file:

Date	3-1	3-2	3-3	3-4	3-5	3-6	3-7	Average per day
Total Visitors from Search Engines (SE)	839	831	774	757	575	438	454	667
Total Unique Visitors	2866	3004	2726	2625	2219	1773	2027	2463
SE Visitors/ Total Visitors								27%

Per Day Averages				
Total SE Visitors (from above)	Total Unique Visitors (from above)	SE Visitors/ Total Visitors (from above)	Sales per day	Sales per day/ Total Visitors
667	2463	27%	32	1.3%

Over a period of time, you will be able to see the emerging relationships between keywords, search engines and sales. Analyzing these relationships will show you where you need to improve your site.

Track visitors with a traffic analyzer. A *unique visitor* is a person that visits your site for the first time. Some statistical reporting programs will tell you unique visitors per 24 hour period. This means, if the visitor returns the next day, they are counted again as a unique visitor, even if they have already been to your site.

When you start to analyze the data, you will be exposed to a lot of numbers. Make sure that you know the difference between the unique visitor and *total hits* on your site. Total hits can be anything from hits on every page to hits on every page and every graphic (total accesses).

You will need to know the number of unique visitors in order to track your sales success.

Simple site statistics usually provided by your host will tell you how many unique visitors your site is getting.

Track Search Engines with a traffic analyzer.
Depending on your site statistics program, you may also be able to see which search engines are referring traffic to your site. You may prefer a more advanced program that will provide graphical charts to represent site traffic.

Don't expect to get every page ranked in every engine. Some search engines just naturally pick up more pages than others. Search engines are always in a competition for who has the biggest database of web pages. You may find that one search engine may be picking up and ranking almost every page of your site, while another engine only likes your home page. It is also dependent on the popularity of the specific search engine.

We've dealt with the statistics for many web sites over many years. We believe that Google sends the most traffic. But that doesn't mean that Google always sends the most quality traffic. Quality traffic (traffic that produces sales) can vary by search engine. One important variable would be the product. For instance, traffic from MSN may bring many sales for your product, whereas traffic from Google may yield you less sales per unique visitor.

You will need to look at your statistics over many months to determine which engines are bringing you sales and which keywords are producing traffic and sales for your specific product.

Track keywords with a traffic analyzer and a ranking report: Again, an advanced program will be very useful to help you accurately track the ranks of specific keyword phrases in the engines. We recommend WebPosition by WebTrends. They offer a free download trial version. (Incidentally, you can also get a traffic analyzer through this software which may help you integrate your statistics.) Although a tad expensive, WebPosition is a good tool for the beginning optimizer. The "Reporter" tool is extremely helpful to analyze how keyword phrases are progressing in rank (or regressing).

There are many other programs available on the market that can provide you with a ranking report. You may also track ranks of specific keywords by hand. Tracking by hand involves going to the search engine and typing in the keywords to see where your site comes up in the ranks.

Whereas WebPosition will provide a ranking report for each search engine for keywords and phrases that you specify, a traffic analyzer like Advanced Logger will tell you the keywords and phrases that people are actually using to find your site. This is an important distinction. For instance, you may have optimized for the keywords "wooden toy boats" and according to your ranking report, you are ranking in the top ten. However, when you study your actual site statistics with your traffic analyzer, you find that people are coming to your site for the phrase "blue toy boats."

Why does this happen? You've chosen to optimize for keywords that no one is searching on. This tells you that you may need to go back to your pages and re-optimize or you may want to leave the pages alone if they are bringing in quality traffic that produces sales.

When you start getting a good amount of traffic (at least 500 unique visitors per week) you will start to understand that the keyword phrases people use are wide and varied. You will notice that you're getting traffic from search engines on phrases that you never thought of. The essence of a good search engine promotion campaign is that you see a nice spread of traffic from ALL engines and a nice spread of keyword phrases.

Some equations that may help you analyze traffic:
Percent Increase of Unique Visitors:
- UVB = unique visitors before a promotion campaign. They should be over a specific period of time, like 4 weeks.
- UVA = unique visitors after or during a promotion campaign. This should be over the same period of time as UVB - 4 weeks.
- UVA - UVB = difference
- Difference/UVA = percent of visitor increase

Percent Increase of Hits from Search Engine(s):
- HB = hits from search engine(s) before a campaign over specific time
- HA = hits from search engines after a campaign over same time period as HB
- HA - HB = difference
- Difference/HA = percent increase of hits from search engine(s)

Percent increase in sales:
- Sales/Unique Visitors = percent of sales/visitors

On the same day of each week (or month) you should calculate your sales/unique visitor ratio. This will tell you if your promotion campaigns are increasing sales, not just visitors. (We'll venture to say that 1% is a good ratio. That is one sale per 100 visitors. If you see anything over 1%, you should examine the campaign and try to replicate it in any way possible.)

Paying For Ranks, Directory Listings, or Spidering

At some point, you may want to consider paying money to get into engines and directories. There are several options for spending your advertising money online:

"Pay-Per-Click." There are several search engines that charge for ranks or listings. Overture and Google Adwords are the two biggest players on this scene. You bid on keywords and you are placed in the list based on your bid. If you are willing to pay enough money per click, you can obtain a number one rank for keyword phrases that you specify.

However, we are not experts in Pay Per Click. The focus of this book is to teach you how to obtain organic listings (listings you don't pay for.) If you are interested in pay-per-click models of SEO, we recommend checking out the SEO ezines and discussion lists in the Resources section at the end of this book. You can also go directly to the above mentioned programs (overture.com and google.com) and read their promotional literature.

If we sound cold about these programs, it's because we've been left with a shivery feeling by Overture. We're not saying that you won't have success. Just, understand that these programs take time to learn, implement, and analyze. And be prepared to spend money during the learning process.

Pay for directory listings. The one directory listing you should pay for is Yahoo. Yahoo will have a direct impact on your search engine ranks. You may also want to research other business directory listings like YellowPages.com.

We are not willing to comment on the effectiveness of other directories as we do not have any proof that they will send you traffic or help your ranks. But we will say that you have to be willing to try new promotion methods. Internet promotion is a wild frontier. You have to be brave enough to take calculated risks. The only way you are going to know if a program will work is to read the promotional literature, dig up further information in discussion lists, and then buy into it in order to test it for your specific product.

Also find directories that are specific to your industry. These directories may not necessarily cost money. It is definitely helpful to your popularity to get listed in a place with similar content. Industry related directories are one such place.

Pay for spidering. Several search engines now have a "Pay for Inclusion" option. This takes the mystery out of wondering when the search engine's spider will come to your site and grab your changes. It's important to realize that in this model, there is no guarantee of rank, only a guarantee that the spider will visit the page that you've paid for and place it in the database of searchable pages.

We see the benefit of paying for inclusion for a new site. However, if you are already in the database, we do not see the benefit of these programs. If you are in the database, the spider will come back to your site eventually. Also realize that if you can get your home page in the database and your link structure is sound, the spiders will find your other pages.

Content Development

Search engine promotion is all about content. Thus, content development will aid in getting more traffic via search engines. Content development means adding new, optimized pages to your web site on a regular basis. Below are several ideas on the types of content you can consider adding to your site.

Develop resource pages. You can add new pages via a "resource section." You will need a section on your site dedicated to this purpose. The resource section might be called *News*, *Articles*, *Resources* or *Information*.

Where can you find information to fill this section? You can write your own content or you can search out free content. Currently, there are many sites that offer free content. In most cases, you are allowed to use this content for your web site, free of charge, if you provide an "author's resource box" with an active link at the end of the article.

An author's resource box looks something like this:

In the Resource section of this book, you will find a list of several web sites that offer free content.

Be sure to optimize every new article that you place on your site. Optimizing articles is very easy. Simply put the title of the article in the <TITLE> tag. Copy the first few lines of the article in the <META NAME="Description"> tag. Put a few keyword phrases from the article into the <META NAME="keywords"> tag. Make sure you have <h2> or <h3> tag that also contains the title of the article. You will learn quickly to look for articles with keywords in the title that relate to your niche.

A live example of an extensive resource section is located here: thewritemarket.com/tools.shtml

Establish web archives for your ezine, webzine or print newsletter. If you write an ezine (newsletter published through email) or a webzine (newsletter published on your web site), or even publish a printed newsletter, you have plenty of fresh content! You can archive that information on your site. You would set up a section of your site dedicated to your ezine or webzine and publish each issue on its own page. Remember to optimize each page the same way you would optimize articles you put into your resource section.

A live example of an archive is located here:
thewritemarket.com/archives.shtml

Add a new page for *every* product. Aside from adding articles and information, if you have several products, even hundreds of products, each product should be on its own web page. Each product page should have a picture, a title, a description and ordering information. Be sure to optimize each page using the steps in the chapter "Writing for Search Engine Promotion." Product pages will work as natural doorways from search engines into your site. They are probably one of the most effective techniques you can use to get qualified traffic to your site.

For examples of product pages start here:
catoctinkettlekorn.com
Click on the "Products" button and click your way through until you find a product page.

Develop a plan for content development. Set aside a few hours on a regular schedule to work on content (like once a week). Strive for at least 100 pages of content. Always remember, the more content you have, the more chances you have for the search engines to find you.

Focus your content. In order to do well in the search engines, keep in mind that you need to add content that focuses on a specific theme or niche. For instance, if you are selling handbags, then your content needs to relate to handbags. Try to keep your content pinpointed on topics that would be of interest to people that are looking for handbags.

The true key to search engine optimization is to keep adding content to your site that focuses on your niche.

Contact

Thank you for reading. If you have any questions, comments, or critiques please send them to:

webadmin@thewritemarket.com

The Write Market
179 Vista Lane
Shenandoah Junction, WV 25442

Checklist

☐ Do you have your own domain name and hosting services?

Design:

☐ Are you using a professionally designed web site template?

☐ Does each page have a consistent look?

Writing:

☐ Are your pages readable – can people easily scan your individual pages to find what they need?

☐ Is your content interesting?

☐ Does your content speak to your customers?

☐ Is all your content focused on a specific topic or niche?

Navigation:

☐ Can a visitor easily find a specific product or specific information on your site?

☐ Can search engine spiders easily find their way around your site?

Optimization:

☐ Are your keywords related to your product or services?

☐ Are you optimizing for keyword phrases not individual keywords?

☐ Have you used the keyword phrase in the title tag?

☐ Have you used the keyword phrase at least three times in the body copy?

Submission:

☐ Did you submit to at least one major search engine?

☐ Did you submit to at least one major directory?

Analysis:

☐ Can you find your site in the major search engines and directories that you submitted to?

☐ Do you have a traffic analyzer?

Content Development:

☐ Have you dedicated a section of your site to add more content?

☐ Do you have a plan to implement content development?

Troubleshooting

These are some tips that will give you a place to start. You may have to go further and do more research on these problems. Check out the Resources section if this Troubleshooting section section doesn't solve your problems.

Flash Introduction

PROBLEM:

Spider cannot get through Flash into the site.

SOLUTION:

Embed the Flash into the page. Have a link into the site in plain HTML.

Frames

PROBLEM:

Spider cannot get past the frame and find the pages of the site.

SOLUTION:

• Utilize the <NOFRAMES> tag on the index or default page of your site. Place links and text within the <NOFRAMES> tag.

• Have a links menu on all of your pages that are to be pulled up in the main page of the frame. A text link menu at the bottom of each page would do the trick. This links menu will allow the spider to find each page of your site.

Programming that brings in content on the fly

PROBLEM:

Spiders cannot find your web pages.

SOLUTION:

• Tell your programmer up front that you need search engine spiders to have the ability to crawl the links. They may have solutions for you.

• If you are working with a site that's already programmed, you can add a link to a site map from the home page. The site map should be a straight HTML page. The site map will contain crawlable links that the search engine can follow. Pages with the extension .ASP and .CFM (ColdFusion) generally will be found by spiders as long as you have a good link structure. Pages that end in .CGI may not be found by spiders because CGI programming sometimes requires a question mark when calling up the page.

Site not listed in a search engine

PROBLEM:

Typing in the domain name (www.yourdomain.com or yourdomain.com) into the search engine does not yield any results.

SOLUTION:

- Submit your main URL to the search engine's "add URL" page.
- Wait at least a month and check again.
- Get a link from another website to your main URL (the link into your site must be on a page that is already in the search engine database and not from a link farm or a FFA page.)
- Are you using any kind of a redirect or flash or any advanced programming on your main page that might hinder the spider? (See Flash Introduction, Frames and/or Programming that brings in content on the fly.) If you are using any of these, consider the workarounds.

Site is in the database but there are no ranks

You know your site is in the database, but you are not seeing any top ten ranks for your keywords.

SOLUTION:

• Wait one month from the time that you have verified that you are in the database.

• After a month, are you sure you have absolutely no ranks? Do you have a tracker that reports referrals? Are there no referrals for any keywords?

• If you are not getting any referrals, have you optimized for very competitive one-word keywords or have you tried for lengthier "keyword phrases." You may need to repeat the chapter *Writing for the Search Engines.*

• Specifically, focus on your keyword selection and the titles of your pages. Are you optimizing for the right keywords? Is your key-word phrase in the title of your page and used at least one time in your body copy?

• You may need to focus on your link popularity. Sometimes, the phrases are so competitive that you will need to seriously focus on obtaining links from other sites.

Site is receiving referrals but no sales

Site is receiving at least 100 unique visitors a day, but there are no sales.

- If you are getting 100 referrals a day, you should be getting at least one sale per week or more. There are several reasons why sales may not be occurring. I will run down the list of possible reasons and you must try to change each variable to see if you can increase sales. However, I recommend that you change one variable per month and then wait it out. Patience and persistence, my friend!

List of variables:
- Are you using the right keywords? Look at your site statistics. What keywords are people coming to your web site for? If they are not related to your products or services, you have a problem. You will need to re-optimize for the right keywords.
- Do you have a professional web design?
- Is your navigation clear?
- Is your writing clear?
- Do you have an online ordering system or a way for your visitors to contact you online or a toll free phone number?
- Do you state your guarantee clearly?
- Do you have testimonials for your product?
- Is your pricing right for your product?

Resources

Books:

- Krug, S., *Don't Make Me Think!* A Common Sense Approach to Web Usability, 2000, New Riders Publishing
- Oliver, D., *Sam's Teach Yourself HTML and XHTML in 24 Hours*, 2001, Sams
- Strunk, White, Osgood, and Angell, *The Elements of Style*, 2000, Allyn & Bacon

Web sites:

- htmlgoodies.com – free tutorials on HTML programming
- keywordcount.com – tool to determine keyword frequency
- overture.com – useful keyword suggestion tool
- bruceclay.com – *Search Engine Relationship Chart*™

Link Popularity:
- checkyourlinkpopularity.com – downloadable program that will allow you to see how popular your web site is
- linkpopularity.com – online program to check your link popularity
- linkpopularitycheck.com – online program to check your link popularity, will allow comparison

SEO ezines:
- Whalen, J., *High Rankings Advisor*, highrankings.com
- Clough, R., *Search Engine Guide*, searchengineguide.com
- Sullivan, D., *Search Engine Watch*, searchenginewatch.com

SEO discussion lists:
- JimWorld.com
- WebmasterWorld.com

Site metrics (web analytics software):
- perlonline.com – Advanced Logger, one time fee
- clicktracks.com – one time fee
- urchin.com – one time fee
- websidestory.com – HitBox, set up fee and monthly fees
- webtrends.com – set up fee and monthly fees

Free Content:

- ideamarketers.com – searchable database of articles, the most recently submitted articles are free.

- goarticles.com – searchable database of free articles.

- groups.yahoo.com – do a search for "free content." You will find several lists that you can subscribe to. You can subscribe to groups that provide very specific article topics depending on what niche of content you want to focus on. The articles will come right to your email box.

Glossary

algorithm: Any formula used within a computer program. Specifically, the way the search engine is programmed to determine ranks.

automatic update: When the search engine spider automatically returns to your site to check for updates.

author's resource box: Information that you place at the end of the article that will contain contact information and biography information about the author of the article.

CGI: Common Gateway Interface, scripts that run between the server and the visitors to your site. Scripts are necessary for many applications including forms for collecting information.

click popularity: An analysis of the use of a site by counting the number of times that it has been visited. This may be broken down by unique clicks within a given period of time or just a count of every click on your web site.

content development: Adding new optimized pages to your web site on a regular basis or modifying existing pages for improved optimization and readability.

crawling: When the spider follows the links around your site - the spider is *crawling* your site. *Crawlability* is the ability of the spider to follow links and get around your site.

directory: A list of sites which has been compiled with some human intervention. Dmoz.org is an example of a directory.

domain name: www.your-domain-name.com We recommend that you purchase your domain name through your host.

doorway pages: AKA "hallway pages" or "entry pages." Pages that are created for specific search engines for specific keywords. Generally, these pages serve no other purpose than to drive traffic from search engines. They are usually spam, crammed with keywords. Doorway pages have pretty much been killed off by most search engines.

dynamic pages: Pages that are created "on the fly." A site with dynamic pages will have a database. Pages are created by pulling information from the database based on the programming of the page, i.e. a catalogue of items for sale on your site.

entry pages: See doorway pages.

ezine or webzine: A newsletter sent via email or posted on a web site, like an online magazine.

FFA: Free-For-All link pages have thousands of links regardless of content. The links are added by means of a program not a human.

Flash: A self contained animation, using primarily vector based shapes (lines and text) that are ideally suited for the internet because of the small file sizes that result. It also allows for "streaming" content (the animation begins to play while the file is still downloading, reducing the apparent wait time).

frames: HTML code that allows certain portions of a page to remain stationary when visitors move from page to page. Generally, a navigation bar may be put in a frame. If a change needs to be made to navigation, one change to the frame will appear on all pages of the site.

Google page rank: Appears as a little green bar on the Google Toolbar. Your Google page rank can vary from 0-10, ten being the highest (good) and zero being the lowest (bad). It is an indication of how well your site will fare in Google listings and is highly influenced by your site's link popularity.

graphical navigation: A navigation scheme for your entire web site that is created using graphics or images rather than text links.

hallway pages: See doorway pages.

heading tags: <h1> <h2> <h3> <h4> <h5> <h6> <h7> HTML tags that make text bigger and bolder.

host: The server (computer) where your web site is stored. You will need to pay monthly or yearly rent for hosting services.

index: The database of web pages for a search engine.

indexing: Occurs when the search engine takes the pages from the database and places them in an order based on the algorithms of that engine. All search engines have different indexing processes because they have different algorithms.

keyword: A word that people type into a search engine in order to find web sites that relate to that word. A query.

keyword density: See keyword frequency.

keyword phrase: Two or three words in a string. Some examples: "educational toys," "children's books," "wooden boats." Generally, a noun (person, place, or thing) and one or two adjectives (words that describe nouns).

keyword proximity: When two or three keywords are placed together, and how close they are to each other. For instance: "educational books" v. "educational children's books" v. "educational children's monster books." You want words to be placed together when you think people might type them into a search engine exactly that way - a keyword phrase.

keyword frequency: (Also termed *keyword density*) The amount of times a keyword or keyword phrase appears in the text of a web page (can also include the keyword in the title, meta tags, and alt tags.) This is usually referred to as a percentage.
Keyword/Total Words in Text=3% or
Keyword/Total Words in Text, Title and Tags=5%

link farms: Sites that contain pages just for the purpose of exchanging links with other sites without concern for content. Usually contains thousands of links added by a program not a human.

link popularity: A search engine will give your site a high link popularity if many other sites link to yours. Many is over 100.

link structure: See navigation. How all the pages of a web site are categorized and linked to each other.

listing: See placement, position, ranks. Your placement in the index of a search engine when someone places a query.

navigation: See link structure. How people will find their way around your site.

on the fly: Information is called up from a database based on the programming of the page.

organic listings: Listings in the search engines that you will not need to pay for. This book is teaching you how to obtain organic listings.

optimization: The process of improving your site to gain ranking or boost ranking of your web pages within search engines.

paid results: When the search engine provides listings that people have paid for. Overture and Google Adwords are currently the biggest providers of paid results.

PPC or Pay-Per-Click: If you pay for each visitor that comes from a search engine, you are paying per click. Several engines now provide paid results. Overture and Google Adwords are currently the biggest providers of PPC campaigns.

placement: See listings, positioning, ranks. Your position in the list a search engine produces when someone places a query.

positioning: Where the search engine puts a web page in relation to other web pages when someone places a query. Generally referred to as a number. For instance: your web page has a number one position on page one. See also placement, listing, ranks.

query: The keywords a person types into a search box. The person is *querying* the search engine.

rank(s): See listings, positioning, placement. Your position in a search engine when someone places a query.

reciprocal links: In this tit for tat situation you provide a link from your site to another site and they provide a link back to your site. You're reciprocating with links.

SEO: Search Engine Optimization – the process of improving your site to gain ranking or boost ranking of your web pages within search engines.

search engine: A series of programs on a server which produce listings of web sites. A search engine is a machine *tuned* by humans to rank web pages. Google is an example of a search engine.

spam: Overuse of the same word in your title, meta tags, or text. Putting words or phrases into your meta tags or title that have nothing to do with the actual content people see on your web page. Pages with the same text but on different domains. A page with strings of keywords and no real content. Shady pages created solely for the purpose of bringing traffic from search engines.

spider: A spider is a program that crawls your site and finds your pages. It then stores those pages in a database for later retrieval by a search engine when someone queries the search engine.

stemming technology: Program code within the search engine that builds derivations of the query. For instance, if you type in "educational," the search engine may bring up results with the word "education."

stop words: You may notice that some search engines do not use words like these in a search: *a, and, the, of, that, it,* and *to.* Those are stop words.

sub navigation: Second or Third level directory of links that people use to delve deeper in your web site.

submission: Asking a search engine to send out their spider to place you in their database. The search engine provides an "add url page" for you to put your URL into.

template: A predefined navigation system, usually composed of graphics, that you can implement on every page of your site for consistency. You can find templates in your favorite search engine by doing a search for "free web site templates."

themes or theming: Focusing the content of your site on a specific niche or topic.

unique visitor: A person that visits your site for the first time. Some statistical reporting programs will tell you unique visitors per 24 hour period. This means, if the visitor returns the next day, they are counted again as a unique visitor, even if they have already been to your site.

URL: Uniform Resource Locator, a domain name, e.g. http://www.thewritemarket.com

Forms

The following forms may be useful in keeping track of certain aspects of the process of optimization. If you only have one web site, we recommend that you write directly in this book, to keep all your optimization records in one place.

If you have several web sites, you may need to develop notebooks for each site. Either way, it is very important to keep a record of the following items.

Keywords and Keyword Phrases

Keywords and Keyword Phrases

_____

_____

_____

_____

_____

_____

_____

_____

_____

_____

_____

_____

_____

_____

_____

_____

_____

_____

_____

_____

_____

_____

_____

Submissions

Date Submitted	Where Submitted	Date Listing Verified

Submissions

Date Submitted	Where Submitted	Date Listing Verified

Printed in the United States
48928LVS00002B/63

9 781581 124729